Old stones and ancient bones

poems from the hollow hills

Gordon MacLellan

First published 2013
Creeping Toad:
www.creepingtoad.org.uk

Text copyright Gordon MacLellan 2013
Photographs copyright Gordon MacLellan
and Susan Greenwood

ISBN 978-1-291-46593-8

Old stones
and ancient bones

Contents

By way of explanation

My work as a storyteller and artist takes me all over the country Wherever I go, I try to visit local woods and ponds, walk beside dark lochs, meet ancient trees, enjoy the sigh of the wave on the shore. And if there are any nearby ancient monuments, I'll often end up inside them. From ruined castles and fallen monasteries to Roman remains and Iron Age forts, I'll enjoy them all. But it is Stone Age sites that draw me most strongly: be it cave, cairn, henge, ring or tomb - or even the vague memory of the line of a track

Most of the poems are written from and about very specific sites but they are also, at least for me, some of my meditation "keys", opening doorways into awareness and I happily change names to link self to place or to shift blessings to seasons. If these words offer you similar opportunities, feel free to improvise! Notes about individual pieces come in at the end.

I am a storyteller, I tend to write words for speaking aloud, so please don't just read; whisper as well, or declaim, or hiss…but whatever you do, even if it is only to kindle a fire with these bits of paper, enjoy.

Gordon the Toad, August 2013
www.creepingtoad.org.uk
www.creepingtoad.blogspot.co.uk

Gannets

Gannets in tight formation
Cutting lines across the waves
Sharp.
Precise as knives.

Invitations
The hills are waiting
Come,
With wolf howl and raven brake,
To the sailing clouds.

Come,
With a knife-edge scream,
The sword thrust of swifts,
An echo of buzzards.

Come with the gale,
Along the ridge galloping,
Come with a windthrow of rooks,
And a solitude of ravens.

Come,
By Axe Edge and Pilsbury
By Beggars Bridge and Crowdicote
By Wolfscote Dale and Ravens Tor.

Du.
Dubh.
Black.
Dove black.
Dove holes.
Dove Dale.
Caves,
Old sockets in a mountain skull,
Moss grown and lichen edged,
Drip, dripping, lime-sodden water, and

Water-sodden stone.

Come,
Dark black,
Stone black,
Flagstone smooth.
Water running,
Hole boring,
Time worn,
Time warm
Limestone.

Come,
By Axe Edge and Pilsbury
By Beggars Bridge and Crowdicote
By Wolfscote Dale and Ravens Tor.

Come,
The hills are waiting

The Satyr's stories: the Waking Song

To moss-grown stone
By fern tongues unrolling,
With nettle's bite,
And pheasant's cry,
Wake.

To gooseberry juice
By towering ivied pine,
With forget-me-not skies
And primrose yellows,
Wake.

To waterfall lullabies
And birdsong cascading,
To chill mornings
And the promise of warmth
Wake.

To arum's broad leaves
And the flight of bumblebees,
When bells ring,
Smoking blue under the trees,
Wake.

Wake
With stonefly and alder,
And the last of the May
As sweet as cream,
Wake.

The Satyr's stories: the Calling Song
With the fire of foxes, come,
With the endurance of limestone, come,
With the persistence of tree roots, come,
With the passion of orchids, come,
With the excitement of children, come.

And where the cliff
Crumbles into the grass;
Past Gilbert's stone
And Sir Henry's Yards;
Past Engine and Portobello and
Sad Molly Wootton's Hole;
Beyond Perch Pit and
Over the Limeyards Flats,

By the cold, carp depths
Of Blackwater
We'll watch the moon rise over Margaret's Close,
and gather the woodland on the dancing lawns at
Ridings Nook.

Being there

Minninglow
Flint.
Fire.
Shadows,

Last memories,
Locked in stone but,
From here
The wide horizon
Is golden

Broch of Gurness, Orkney
Stacked.
Stone slabs with drystone care.
From Neolithic village to Pictish broch
To modern pebble-dashed croft,
Resource and response
Remain the same.
The wind still blows.
The sea still rushes the shore.
The sunset still glows across the clouds and burns
the world into light.

Tomb of the Eagles

To be chosen to lie
In bone on stone
For generations,
Was that the honour,
A privilege;
Or an obligation?
To wait down the centuries,
Appeased with gravegoods, but
Bound in stone,
Questioned, petitioned,
And left behind until,
I arrive with a metal light
And listen for your whisper in
The broken dark

Or did freedom in death
Wait for the flaying
By eagles,

A used skull picked clean
And tumbled off the cliff edge,
Into the sea.
Did a freedom of soul
Wait for the wind,
Or the wave, and
A chance to turn and run again
In fur, in feather, in family skin?

Bitter

This plexiglass sunlight will fade,
And this cold, subterranean chill will drain those
batteries,
And then your integrity will be tested
By your own smoking candle-stub,
And our hungry, eye-socket darkness

Waiting

Caring nothing for sun and moon,
Seasons, stars and centuries,
Our lady of rock, flame and darkness,
Huge, round, stone-shaped into flesh,
The Old Stone Woman,
Waits

Hunter

Bone leaves me breathless,
The sweep and spike of antler,
In the flared hands of a fallow buck.
Rattling against stone, against branch,
Against the doors of my soul

Shaman

Twist, turn, shake, whirl,

The dancer turns, breathes and
The wild wind winnows
The soul from the flesh

Long flight of the swallow
Poised, trembling, then tilting
With the world falling away

Dancing the layers of the landscapes,
Feeling the secretive stories of stones,
Through feet and tears and beating blood

Until I am driven,
Blown hard back into
Flesh and warm bone,
Falling again to the waking world,
Dancing

Camster

How well did we build for our Dead?
These stones, so carefully chosen, carefully
stacked,
Hand by hand,
Muscle, bone and determination.
A passage, a chamber to face the sunrise

> *Here we rest,*
> *Here we lie,*
> *Bodies taken by fire and wind*
> *Our bones charred to hold memories*
> *Not just mine and yours and ours, but*
> *everyone's*
> *All of our people, soaked into our bones*
> *Sunk into these stones*
> *Tales not told in so many years*

How well do the Dead receive us?
In these beautiful chambers,
Rooms that ring with voices, with song, with
chanted prayer,
A close tunnel, a crawl under watchful spaces
Into this room that holds the voices of the Dead.
A cist to contain and a cist to be contained within,
Stone slabs that hold me, a thrill of contact, of
connection.
A place to stop, to sing,
To be still in the darkness,
To listen for the sunrise

Socket

The sweep of the sky,
The rain's bow,
The curl of a wave,
The sand's dune,
All contained in
The scoop of an eye's socket,
And the bowl of a skull.
A world cradled in
My electric palms

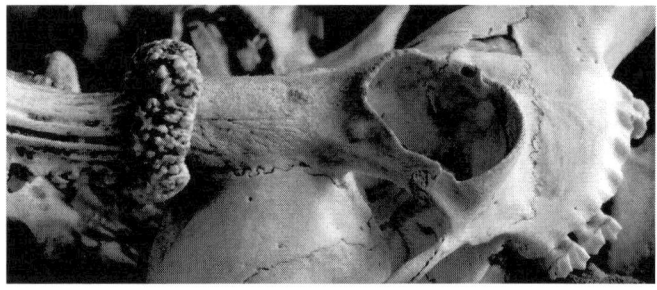

The Bone Pit

A drumming thunder of running hooves, a racing
sweep over the hilltops.
Steaming breath, rolling eyes, the wind flare of
mane.
The heart beats quicker, hooves before paws, before
claws, before teeth.

> *Remember those who have gone.*
> *Bone upon bone,*
> *Rattle and fall,*
> *Tooth and horn,*
> *Fang and jaw,*
> *Warm flesh, fur and feather all grow cold*
> *Together in the bone-pit darkness*

And wait.
Wait for a pick, for a shovel and a gentle touch
To lift the darkness of 10,000 years.

10,000 years is not so long.
We can look up and out, beyond these Buxton walls
And see the hills the old animals saw.
The folded dales may remember them yet and
All those we have lost may
Still walk in the dreams the land is dreaming.

> *Aurochs, giant deer, bear, lion, and*
> *mastodon,*
> *Remember those who have gone.*
> *Bone upon bone,*
> *Rattle and fall,*

Tooth and horn,
Fang and jaw,
Warm flesh, fur and feather all grow cold
Together in the bone-pit darkness

Blessings

Brodgar
Slip into stillness
Beside a tall stone
Bristled and bearded with
lichen.

Listen to the voices that
Whisper along the wind,
Through the grass,
Out of the old stone itself,
Saying,

Power of the raven,
Power of the rain on the hills,
Power of the wind over the
moor,
Power of the hare in the grass
Be thine.

Grace of the clover,
Grace of the geese in the loch,
Grace of the gunmetal grey
clouds,
Grace of the white clouds that
catch the light
Be thine

Stillness of the wave on the shore,
Stillness of stone in the Ring,
Stillness of sunrise behind the ridges,
Stillness of long sleep in the hollow hills
Be thine

Strength of the gull's freedom,
Strength of the bull's endurance,
Strength of the rooks' gathering,
Strength of the crab's stealth
Be thine

May no day be grievous to thee,
May each day be joyous to thee,
May love of each face be thine
May death on pillow be thine,
Honour and compassion.

Wyrd

Feel the patterns of the world
Whirling out from this hub,
This womb, this cave, this void.
Webs,
The knotted threads
Of fishing nets

> *Wave to stream,*
> *Rock to pebble,*
> *Eagle to fish,*
> *Raven to ram,*
> *Deed to deed,*
> *Life to death.*
> *Thought to dream.*

Those three old women
Sitting in the hollow dark of the hill,
Spinning the world,
From dreaming to waking

Anticipation, 1

Behind every moment,
Behind every movement,
In the lifting air under the gull's wing,
In the spaces between the falling leaves,
In the bursting bud,
In the endless flow of water over stone,
In clouds sailing into the blue,
In the foraging path of a honey bee.

In the emptiness
After the cutting scream of a swift

Stillness waits

Anticipation, 2

Autumn waits,
Falling into gold, and yellow, and russet,
As mist gathers,
Wool unravelled through the trees.
In the hollow dales,
The lake anticipates winter,
And the rune-cracked ice.
But for now,
Its dark, cold reflective depth
Is divination enough

Faerie
On Law Hill

They always say you should never...
Early autumn, mid-day and safely,
I went for a walk

An east wind blowing, long and cold
Over flat lands with a distant taste of the sea

Scots Pine sigh like a shore
Receiving waves.
The grass moves,
A round hill breathing peace

They always say you should never.....

I leant against a tree-trunk and
Let my worries go,
Feeding them as leaves to the wind

I let them go
(They always say...)
I let it all go
(They always say you should never...)
Debt, doubt, despair, despondency,
The wind took them for me
And left.
*(They said. They always said. Who ever
listens...)*

Ever now,

Never now,
Ever and for always,
Old stone and tree-roots,
I am sitting here still.

And you…
You may choose a spring morning,
(Please don't sleep, don't snooze in the...)
Stones warmed on the edge of summer.
Sitting back, leaning back,
Slipping gently, warmly,
Comfortably into sleep.
An afternoon snooze,
Endless dozing,
(Don't...)

Rest your back against me,
Listen to the trees speaking peace.

You may prefer a frosty noon when,
(Inviting rest, Faerie Hills and Faerie Hollows)
Sun melting invites a rest or
A fey midsummer with heat shimmering the
distance,
(They said, they said, too late, they said...)

But rest, just rest, a while.
Settle.
Slide down the stone beside me.
Slide into stone beside me.

The Satyr's stories: beginning

I was born out of the need of old stone and tree
roots for a voice.

I was as an idea, shaped by water running through
stone in deep caves, gathering a body for myself
out of long lost bones, out of stranded horns and
hooves and left-over memories. My flesh is earth,
my skin grass and bark, my blood the mineral rich,
crystal-growing streams of limestone darkness.

Now I am here, playing the music of the wind,
listening to bluebells ring,
the slow singing of carp in the cold pools.
I am the watcher in the woods,
The touch of the breeze,
The rustle in the undergrowth.

I am the shadow that slips away.

Kelpie

Water,
Peat brown, tea brown
Staining mugs,
Baths.
Tanning skin.
Glowing golden, rushing,
Brown with life, spilling out of the moors
Off the purple-heathered muir-burn hills.

Rushes spiked and quivering,
Moss swallowing wood and stone,
And the body that sinks in the peat-bog wallow.

Feel the cold,
Moss-pickled branches, pickled bones,
Drowned twig fingers
To comb the weeds from my hair,
The dream of the Kelpie in a dark pool.

The Ford

Warm stones
Worn hollow with the years
A sunken path
Dipping between trees to the ford
An old story on this old path

> *The blood flows,*
> *Axe edge,*
> *Shield rim,*
> *Spear throw,*
> *Splitten sinew and*
> *Broken bone*

And the Washer watches
As the water runs clear

Skull saved, bones polished
Laid aside with care
To be lost in the heather and the hills

The river remembers,
Not in this water
That rushes, laughing, towards the sea
But here,
In this ripple repeated,
That fall,
The pool.
Memory and sorrow
In swirl and pebble,
And Shellycoat is left alone again

Farewell
Why bother?

Why? Why bother?
Old stones and dusty bones
Hellfire and pagan damnation
Attend these ungodly things

But tombs are a pledge,
A commitment to the future,
The might have,
They did,
Use wood and peat and grass
And nothing at all.
But they also wrapped their dead in stone
And they cared enough
To enter their people
Into these hills, these glens
Into the sea that even then was eating the land.
Endurance,
A lasting enchantment,
Believing enough
To trust their dead to
These landscapes
And believing enough to
Trust this land to their watchful dead

And somehow these
Stargazers, travellers, mathematicians
Artists, builders, hunters,
Fishers, farmers, families

Believed in us enough
To leave their Dead
Under our awkward feet

A legacy of hope,
Descendants of place and passion
And maybe somewhere some slight
Thread of persistent DNA

Why bother?
Because they did.

Gannets, 2

Foam trails ripple
Across a whale-dark sea,
While precise, sharp and white,
Gannets glide in fleeting runes
Across the lines on the pages of the waves.

Old stones and ancient bones Notes

1. Invitations

These three poems are drawn from specific places but they all invite you to step out and into your own wild places. These are not remote wildernesses. The hills and dales in *The Hills Are Waiting* are in the Peak District: within 60 minutes drive of about half the population of England and a landscape worn and harried by humans for centuries. (Du and Dubh (pro *doo* and *doov*) both mean black and probably gave the "Dove" of Dovedale.) The other two poems were both first written for a project for the National Trust at Calke Abbey. They grew out of the Limeyards: limestone quarries only abandoned in the last century and reclaimed with vigour and beauty by wood, water and wildflowers. These are two of the Satyr's Stories who you will meet again later

Places:
Dovedale, Derbyshire/Staffordshire, Peak District
Limeyards: Calke Abbey, Ticknall, Derbyshire

2. Being there

Minninglow: an atmospheric and windswept Neolithic burial ground on a ridge in the Peak District.
Tomb of the Eagles: such a stunning place in such a stunning setting. That sense of a huge world

waiting outside that low, dark entrance really made me wonder which was the privilege: to be entombed or to be left for the eagles to pick your bones and leave them on the rocks or to have them tumble into the sea – even if the sea was a good bit further away than it is now. Maybe to be set in a tomb, was a mark of respect, an honour accorded with attendant gifts but also an obligation. To be cairn-bound might have you soul-bound as well

Bitter, Waiting, Hunter: and who knows what is waiting for you in the dark places of the hollow hills? And have you seen those (presumed) antler-head-pieces found in some caves and cairns? No? Well go and have a look. Image: from the Tomb of the Eagles

Shaman: who knows what it was like for our ancestors, 'way back then but certainly this is what it is like for me now. I hope there is an echo

Camster: from the Grey Cairns of Camster. There is a chamber there that rings with voices

The Bone-pit: an extract from a longer audio-trail poem, *Time Move On* for *The Wonders of the Peak* exhibition in Buxton Museum and Art Gallery

Places:
Minninglow: near Pikehall, Derbyshire
Broch of Gurness, Mainland, Orkney
Tomb of the Eagles, South Ronaldsay, Orkney
Grey Cairns of Camster, near Lybster, Caithness

3. Blessings

Brodgar: it was just like that, a wet windy morning, with the sun escaping clouds occasionally

32

and the voices of the stones whispering blessings. This form is an old one (take a look at Alexander Carmichael's *Carmina Gadelica*)...the strengths of the blessing might change with your own situation: let the place and the moment bless you rather than images that belonged to a distant island and a distant time. The final verse comes straight from the Carmina G

Wyrd: not sure if this is a blessing. It feels like one to me! A blessing of awareness. And before someone gets pedantic and starts telling me that Wyrd as a word and thought belongs with later Norse and Germanic peoples, yes. So what? I met three old women spinning life, death and nightmares in the hollow of a hill and I wouldn't dream of arguing with them

Anticipation 1 and 2: these aren't particularly bound to ancient sites, more a sense of being in the world and a part of its timelessness, For how many thousand years have bees buzzed and swifts screamed over our hills and rivers and coasts?

Places:

Ring of Brodgar, Mainland, Orkney

4. Faerie

Often the tumuli of the ancestors become the Faerie Hills of later stories. Not always. The Good Neighbours themselves are often quite careful to distinguish between *their* hollow hills and *our* hollow hills

Law Hill in Clackmannanshire is a beautiful, haunted place, maybe one thing or the other or both or neither. Whichever, whatever, it seduces

Beginning: this is the satyr of the Limeyards woods who sang the Waking Song and the Calling Song. A dear friend, who I don't meet nearly often enough. Also a little homage here to Jim Henson's ***Dark Crystal***
Kelpie: the Kelpie has a very dubious reputation but is also (another) very old friend (at least for me)
The ford: out of Highland Scottish folklore, "The Washer at the Ford" washes rags stained red with the blood of those who are about to die and Shellycoat is a rather sad Boggart dressed in shells and weeds who loiters on riverbanks...

5. Farewell
Why bother? A muttering, grumpy old man sort of poem. They left their Dead where we could find them, visit them. How could we not care – for those who have gone, for their Dead who remain, for all of us who are their descendants in this land – even if only because we walk where they did. How we care for the Dead – theirs or our own – might be a reflection of how we care for the living
Gannets: if ever you get the chance, just watch these birds

Photo credits
Cover, Bitter, Gannets 2: Susan Greenwood
All other images by Gordon MacLellan

Printed in Great Britain
by Amazon